Writing the Critical Essay

ABORTION

An  OPPOSING VIEWPOINTS® Guide

Writing the Critical Essay

ABORTION

An OPPOSING VIEWPOINTS® Guide

Other books in the Writing the Critical Essay series:

Writing the Critical Essay

ABORTION

An **OPPOSING** **VIEWPOINTS®** Guide

Mary E. Williams, *Book Editor*

Christine Nasso, *Publisher*
Elizabeth Des Chenes, *Managing Editor*

OPPOSING
VIEWPOINTS®
SERIES

GREENHAVEN PRESS

An imprint of Thomson Gale, a part of The Thomson Corporation

THOMSON
™
GALE

Detroit • New York • San Francisco • New Haven, Conn. • Waterville, Maine • London

For more information, contact
Greenhaven Press
27500 Drake Rd.
Farmington Hills, MI 48331-3535
Or you can visit our Internet site at http://www.gale.com

LIBRARY OF CONGRESS CATALOGING-IN-PUBLICATION DATA

Abortion / Mary E. Williams, book editor.
   p. cm. — (Writing the critical essay)
  Includes bibliographical references and index.
  ISBN-13: 978-0-7377-3576-5 (lib : alk. paper)
  ISBN-10: 0-7377-3576-7 (lib : alk. paper)
  1. Abortion. 2. Abortion—Moral and ethical aspects. I. Williams, Mary E., 1960–
II. Series.
  HQ767.A153 2007
  179.7'60973—dc22

                          2006043592

Printed in the United States of America

Examining the state of writing and how it is taught in the United States was the official purpose of the National Commission on Writing in America's Schools and Colleges. The commission, made up of teachers, school administrators, business leaders, and college and university presidents, released its first report in 2003. "Despite the best efforts of many educators," commissioners argued, "writing has not received the full attention it deserves." Among the findings of the commission was that most fourth-grade students spent less than three hours a week writing, that three-quarters of high school seniors never receive a writing assignment in their history or social studies classes, and that more than 50 percent of first-year students in college have problems writing error-free papers. The commission called for a "cultural sea change" that would increase the emphasis on writing for both elementary and secondary schools. These conclusions have made some educators realize that writing must be emphasized in the curriculum. As colleges are demanding an ever-higher level of writing proficiency from incoming students, schools must respond by making students more competent writers. In response to these concerns, the SAT, an influential standardized test used for college admissions, required an essay for the first time in 2005.

Books in the Writing the Critical Essay: An Opposing Viewpoints Guide series use the patented Opposing Viewpoints format to help students learn to organize ideas and arguments and to write essays using common critical writing techniques. Each book in the series focuses on a particular type of essay writing—including expository, persuasive, descriptive, and narrative—that students learn while being taught both the five-paragraph essay as well as longer pieces of writing that have an opinionated focus. These guides include everything necessary to help students research, outline, draft, edit, and ultimately write successful essays across the curriculum, including essays for the SAT.

Using Opposing Viewpoints

This series is inspired by and builds upon Greenhaven Press's acclaimed Opposing Viewpoints series. As in the parent series, each book in the Writing the Critical Essay series focuses on a timely and controversial social issue that provides lots of opportunities for creating thought-provoking essays. The first section of each volume begins with a brief introductory essay that provides context for the opposing viewpoints that follow. These articles are chosen for their accessibility and clearly stated views. The thesis of each article is made explicit in the article's title and is accentuated by its pairing with an opposing or alternative view. These essays are both models of persuasive writing techniques and valuable research material that students can mine to write their own informed essays. Guided reading and discussion questions help lead students to key ideas and writing techniques presented in the selections.

The second section of each book begins with a preface discussing the format of the essays and examining characteristics of the featured essay type. Model five-paragraph and longer essays then demonstrate that essay type. The essays are annotated so that key writing elements and techniques are pointed out to the student. Sequential, step-by-step exercises help students construct and refine thesis statements; organize material into outlines; analyze and try out writing techniques; write transitions, introductions, and conclusions; and incorporate quotations and other researched material. Ultimately, students construct their own compositions using the designated essay type.

The third section of each volume provides additional research material and writing prompts to help the student. Additional facts about the topic of the book serve as a convenient source of supporting material for essays. Other features help students go beyond the book for their research. Like other Greenhaven Press books, each book in the Writing the Critical Essay series includes bibliographic listings of relevant periodical articles, books, Web sites, and organizations to contact.

Writing the Critical Essay: An Opposing Viewpoints Guide will help students master essay techniques that can be used in any discipline.

Background to Controversy: When Does Life Begin?

Since its legalization in 1973, abortion continues to be one of the most volatile issues in the United States. Competing groups, which include politicians, activists, religious parties, state legislatures, and judges, are still fighting to increase or to restrict access to the controversial procedure. At the heart of this heated struggle is a fundamental disagreement on when life begins.

Differences of Opinion

Abortion opponents, who often identify themselves as "pro-life," argue that life begins at conception, when a sperm fertilizes an egg cell. Fertilization, they contend, creates a separate individual with a complete genetic code that is distinct from the mother's. Thus, for pro-lifers, the embryo is fully human. They see abortion as the killing of an unborn child and a denial of the basic right to life that the already-born enjoy. As pro-life advocate Carolyn C. Gargaro maintains, "The fetus is a completely separate life from the woman . . . it is not just part of the mother's body. It is temporarily residing there, and birth is just the change of residence [for] an already living, active, person. Just because the unborn is dependent on the mother for nine months, does that give anyone the right to choose to end its life? Being dependent on others should not deprive a helpless human being the fundamental right to live."[1]

Supporters of abortion rights, on the other hand, usually agree that a fertilized human egg is alive. But these "pro-choice" advocates see the embryo as a *potential*

11

individual—they do not believe that it is a living person with rights. Since it is unable to survive outside of the womb, they argue that the embryo should not be seen as a being that is separate from the mother's body. As radio commentator Leonard Peikoff explains, the embryo "is a mass of protoplasm [that] exists as a part of a woman's body. It is not an independently existing, biologically formed organism, let alone a person. That which lives within the body of another can claim no right against its host. Rights belong only to individuals, not to . . . parts of an individual."[2]

Deciding Whether the Unborn Count as People

In the 1973 case of *Roe v. Wade*, the case that made abortion legal in the United States, the Supreme Court proclaimed that the word "person" in the constitution had no "possible prenatal application." In other words, the unborn are not legally defined as people. However, the Court also ruled that when a fetus becomes viable, the state must consider its concerns. A viable fetus is one that has reached the point of being able to survive outside of the womb. So, while first-trimester abortions have been declared legal, states are allowed to restrict access to abortions involving viable fetuses because they are far enough along to potentially survive on their own.

Giving states the power to restrict some types of abortion stirred further debate on when personhood begins. Some abortion opponents argue that if the lives of viable fetuses are protected in some states, they are being treated as persons and should be given the legal status of persons. Furthermore, as abortion opponents point out, birth may occur any time after the sixth month of pregnancy. Since premature infants can live outside of the womb, they argue, abortions of six- or seven-month-old fetuses should be illegal. And as medical technology improves, even younger fetuses may soon be able to survive outside of the mother's body. Many abortion opponents even argue that the question of viability misses the point. A

fertilized egg, if left to grow of its own accord, usually develops into a full-term baby. Therefore, they say, embryos should be seen as living beings that deserve all the rights and protections of human personhood.

In response to pro-life arguments, pro-choice advocates point out that most abortions occur during the early weeks of pregnancy, when the embryo is a simple clump of cells. Even in the case of later-occurring abortions, however, these advocates question whether a fetus should have rights over an already-born person. As pro-choice commentator Brian McKinley contends, "You cannot have two entities with equal rights occupying one body. In the case of a pregnant woman, giving a 'right to life' to the potential person in the womb automatically cancels out the mother's right to Life, Liberty, and the Pursuit of Happiness."[3]

Women demand abortion rights at a rally in 1971, two years before the Roe v. Wade *Supreme Court decision repealed antiabortion laws.*

At a 2006 rally in South Dakota, women hold signs displaying both pro-choice and antiabortion sentiments.

If carrying a fetus ends up endangering a pregnant woman's life, for example, should the fetus's life be preferred over the mother's? The pro-choice response to this question would be no. By defining personhood as being already born, such battles between "fetal rights" and "mothers' rights" are avoided, and the decision to give birth remains a woman's choice.

A Continuing Controversy

For the time being, the debate over personhood and abortion shows no sign of subsiding. As this volume goes to press, several groups have initiated challenges to *Roe v. Wade* in hopes that the Supreme Court will reconsider its legality. Only the future will determine how this controversy plays out.

Whatever becomes of *Roe v. Wade*, abortion is bound to remain one of America's most conflict-ridden issues. The writings in this book offer further exploration of this politically charged topic. Through skill-building exercises and thoughtful discussion questions, students will formulate their own ideas about abortion and develop tools to craft their own essays on the subject.

Notes

1. Carolyn C. Gargaro, "My Views as a Pro-Life Woman," www.gargaro.com/abortion.html, February 5, 2000.
2. Leonard Peikoff, "Abortion Rights Are Pro-Life," www.aynrand.org, January 17, 2003.
3. Brian Elroy McKinley, "Why Abortion Is Moral," http://elroy.net/ehr/abortionanswers.html, 2000.

**Section One:
Opposing
Viewpoints
on Abortion**

Abortion Should Remain Legal

Louise Paul

Louise Paul is a health care and women's rights activist who lives in Philadelphia, Pennsylvania. In the following article she argues that access to abortion must remain legal. She describes how before abortion was legalized in the 1970s, American women had to travel abroad or undergo life-threatening procedures to end unwanted pregnancies. Legalized abortion now offers safe and accessible health care to all women. Furthermore, politicians and judges should not be making decisions about a woman's reproductive life, Paul maintains. She concludes that a woman's choice to have or not to have children is a right that the government should protect.

Consider the following questions:

1. According to the author, why did Sherry Finkbine seek an abortion in 1962?
2. How did older women and married women deal with unplanned pregnancies when abortion was illegal, according to Paul?
3. What are some of the factors that working women face when dealing with pregnancy, according to the author?

Legislation governing reproduction is dangerous to us all, unless it assures an individual the right to make decisions privately and without interference, and to receive reproductive care in safe, legal circumstances. A woman's right to carry a pregnancy to term is protected, just as her right to have an abortion is, when the line

Louise Paul, "We Refuse to Go Back!" *People's Weekly World*, April 24–30, 2004, p. 13. www.pww.org. Reproduced by permission.

Believing that women and not government should decide reproductive issues, these pro-choice demonstrators march in Washington, D.C., in 2004.

of privacy is drawn at the door to the doctor's office, the clinic or Planned Parenthood.

Those who march on Washington [at pro-choice rallies] are marching so that all women can have access to safe, effective health care, whether it is birth control, prenatal care, quality obstetric and gynecologic care, or abortion. We are marching so that women can choose to have large families, small families or no families, and so that laws do not interfere with any of these highly personal choices.

The Bad Old Days

I recall the bad old days. The name Sherry Finkbine, an Arizona mother of four, hit the headlines in 1962 when she sought a safe, legal abortion to avoid delivering a severely handicapped child. She had taken the drug Thalidomide, known to cause severe birth defects, in the first trimester of her pregnancy. She challenged the anti-abortion laws of the time. Unsuccessful in this challenge, she went to Sweden for an abortion. She was fortunate to have the resources to be able to travel and have an abortion under safe, sanitary conditions with trained professionals to carry out the procedure.

In the 1970s individual states, New York being the first, passed laws making abortions legal. *Roe v. Wade* soon followed.

As with abortion, birth control has not always been legal. Pioneers in delivering birth control risked arrest and jail in the late 19th and early 20th centuries. Even after it became available to married couples, it was not until years later that birth control was available to teens and young, unmarried adults. Everyone I knew in high school who became pregnant either got married, or "went to live with an aunt" in another town and put her baby up for adoption. Occasionally, a really brave young woman would not get married, and kept her baby, raising it by herself or with the help of her parents. If the young woman chose to keep her baby, whether she married or not, her education was almost always cut short,

Dan Wasserman. Reproduced by permission.

or interrupted. Prior to *Roe v. Wade*, women risked life or permanent injury with illegal abortions.

Even with birth control, older women and married women also had to deal with unwanted or unplanned pregnancies. I can remember a friend saying her mother had tried rolling off the couch to induce a miscarriage. Another had tried large doses of laxatives. Family doctors were approached to perform abortions, but risked their medical licenses and livelihoods. Doctors were not willing to do tubal ligations for women who had decided their families were complete. This sterilization procedure eventually became more common, but a woman's husband had to give written permission. If a medical reason could be found, a woman could have a hysterectomy, which also produces sterilization but is a much more complicated operation.

A woman carries a sign demanding abortion rights at a protest against the closing of a Wisconsin abortion clinic in 1971.

Supporting Women's Decisions

All women strive to realize their potential as humane, capable, intelligent beings. Each woman comes to reproduction with her own set of beliefs, religious and otherwise, with her own set of standards of what is humane and what is not, and her own life circumstances. When faced with pregnancy, women have to consider their own lives and the lives of other family members. For working women, these are matters of continuing employment, of putting food on the table, and of providing shelter for themselves and their children. The reproductive decisions based on these circumstances are not to be judged by politicians and legislative or judicial bodies.

We all want some degree of choice over reproduction, whether it be the right to have as many children as we want, the right not to have children, the right to use birth control, the right to space our children, the right to prenatal care, the right to have or not have an abortion. These rights are only guaranteed by agreeing that women, with the advice of their health-care providers, are the decision makers, and by providing safe, competent health care for all of a woman's health-care needs.

Analyze the essay:

1. One persuasive technique this author uses in her essay is to describe the kinds of difficulties women faced before the legalization of abortion and birth control. In your opinion, is this technique effective? Why or why not?

2. The author argues that a woman and her health care provider should be the decision makers when it comes to abortion. Do you agree or disagree? Explain your reasoning.

Abortion Should Not Be Allowed

Daniel Oliver

In this essay Daniel Oliver argues that abortion should not be legal. He explains that the main issue in the abortion controversy is whether a fetus is a person—but neither civilization nor science have ever come up with a definitive answer. Given this uncertainty, Oliver believes that it is better to "play it safe" when it comes to fetal life. Since it is *possible* that the fetus is a person, he concludes, abortion should not be allowed, on the grounds that it would be the same as surgical murder.

Oliver is a senior director at the White House Writers Group in Washington, D.C.

Consider the following questions:

1. According to Oliver, what did the U.S. Supreme Court decide in the 1973 case of *Roe v. Wade*?
2. What guidance does science offer on the status of a fetus, according to the author?
3. What is the Precautionary Principle, according to the author?

The proabortion and antiabortion forces are warships passing in the night. Their slogans, "pro-choice" and "pro-life," don't engage the central issue that divides them, which is, what actually happens in an abortion. Neither group really disagrees with the other's slogan. None of the opponents of abortion would object to a

Daniel Oliver, "Deciding Abortion," *National Review*, vol. LVII, May 9, 2005, pp. 225–26. Copyright © 2005 by National Review, Inc., 215 Lexington Avenue, New York, NY 10016. Reproduced by permission.

woman's choosing to do what she wanted with a tumor or some other unwanted tissue growing on or in her body. On that issue they would be pro-choice. And no ordinary supporter of abortion would argue that a woman has a right to choose to do what she wants with her grandmother, or her infant daughter. In those cases, they would be pro-life, not pro-choice.

Nor was "choice"—understood as a woman's right to choose to terminate the life of a person—authorized by the Supreme Court in *Roe v. Wade*. What the Court decided in that case was that during the period before the fetus was viable (which the Court, writing in 1973, said usually occurred at 28 weeks but could occur earlier, even at 24 weeks) a woman could not be prohibited from exercising her "right to privacy"—which included choosing

Michael Ramirez. Reproduced by permission.

In a 2006 march in San Francisco, this woman joins other abortion opponents in protesting the 33rd anniversary of Roe v. Wade.

to have an abortion. The Court did not hold that a woman had an unqualified right to destroy something that was a person. . . .

Neither "life" nor "choice," therefore, is really the issue in the abortion dispute. . . .

The Central Issue

The first and central issue in the abortion debate is whether the fetus is a person. The second issue is how we should behave if we can't conclusively decide the first issue. Is a fetus a person or simply part of the body of the woman in which it resides? What is life or personhood, and when does it begin? . . .

Two places we could look to for guidance in making that determination are tradition and science. Civilized states have for generations considered the fetus a person. But that tradition is often regarded as suspect—a vestige of religious morality in the post-religious polity. Science also turns out not to be much help. The issue in dispute is not whether that-which-is-growing-inside-the-woman, at whatever stage it has reached (and for simplicity's sake I will call that entity a "fetus"), is some kind of life. Science agrees it is alive and that it has the DNA of the human species, and DNA distinct from its mother's. . . . Science itself does not tell us whether the fetus is a person.

If neither tradition nor science can tell us whether the fetus is a person, what should guide us in deciding whether to allow abortions? What should we do when we don't know something and have no way of figuring it out? We need to find a secular principle that will guide our behavior. . . .

A Thought Experiment

Let's try a thought experiment. Suppose a building is to be demolished as part of a program to construct free housing for the poor. Millions of dollars and many months have been spent preparing for the demolition of the building. Any additional delay, by even a single hour, will result in huge costs. The building has been carefully inspected to be sure that no one is in it. Demolition Day arrives, but moments before the explosive charges are to be detonated, a bystander cries out that he has spotted a figure moving at a window. A dozen others saw something too—but all agree that what they saw was a dog. Does demolition proceed? Probably, unless the animal-rights people can find an accommodating judge to block it. At the very least, the many millions spent and the benefits pending would be weighed against the life of the dog.

> ## A Unique Person
>
> At conception, a unique, self-possessed human person comes into being.
>
> Dan Kennedy, "At the Heart of Cloning," *Life Principles Reflections*, Winter 2002.

Members of a pro-life organization, these young people gather for the 2004 March for Life in Washington, D.C.

But now suppose a dozen different people, all credible citizens, say they were watching the same window and are certain that what they saw was not a dog, but a small boy. What would be done? Can there be any doubt? If there were any chance that the life seen in the building was human, demolition would not proceed. The millions spent would count for nothing. Everyone would apply an innate "precautionary principle" and not accept the risk of killing a human being.

We Cannot Take the Chance

The Precautionary Principle is currently being used by many to counter the current presumption in favor of developing new technologies and products. The Precautionary Principle states that scientific certainty of harm is not required as a prerequisite for taking action to avert it. The most widely cited version of this principle in the environmental context is Principle 15 of the 1992 Rio Declaration on Environment and Development: "Where there are threats of serious or irreversible damage, lack of full scientific certainty shall not be used as a reason for postponing cost-effective measures to prevent environmental degradation."

That sentence applied to the abortion debate would read, "If there is a chance that a human being may be irreversibly damaged by an abortion, lack of certainty about the personhood of the fetus shall not be used as a reason for allowing abortions."

In the case of demolishing the building, in our thought experiment, the precautionary principle that resides in each of us would lead us all to opt for life: If in doubt, take no chance of killing a human being. Isn't that the situation with abortion?

Analyze the essay:

1. Do you agree with the author that because there is no way to prove whether or not the fetus is a person, abortion should not be allowed? Explain your answer.

2. At the end of his essay Oliver uses a "thought experiment," which entails an example about whether or not a building should be demolished if people disagreed about seeing a person inside the building. Is this imaginary scenario effective as a persuasive technique? Why or why not?

Parental Consent Should Be Required for Minors' Abortions

Marcia Carroll

It should be illegal for minors to have an abortion without parental approval, argues Marcia Carroll in the following selection. Parents are responsible for their children's health and should know when they are undergoing medical procedures, she contends. Carroll's teenage daughter became pregnant and initially chose to have the baby. Yet without Carroll's approval, her daughter's boyfriend's family took her to have an abortion in a state that did not require parental permission. The girl later regretted terminating the pregnancy. Carroll urges Congress to pass a law that would require doctors to obtain parental consent before performing abortions on minors.

Consider the following questions:

1. What three things did Carroll find disturbing about the family of her daughter's boyfriend?
2. How old does a minor have to be to have an abortion in Pennsylvania, according to the author?

On Christmas Eve 2004, my daughter informed me she was pregnant. I assured her I would seek out all resources and help that was available. As her parents, her father and I would stand beside her and support any decision she made. . . .

Marcia Carroll, testimony in support of HR 748, the Child Interstate Abortion Notification Act, U.S. House of Representatives, Subcommittee on the Constitution, March 3, 2005.

My daughter chose to have the baby and raise it. My family fully supported my daughter's decision to keep her baby and offered her our love and support.

The Boyfriend's Family

Subsequently, her boyfriend's family began to harass my daughter and my family. They started showing up at our house to express their desire for my daughter to have an abortion. When that did not work, his grandmother started calling my daughter without my knowledge. They would tell her that if she kept the baby, she couldn't see her boyfriend again. They threatened to move out of state.

I told his family that my daughter had our full support in her decision to keep the baby. She also had the best doctors, counselors, and professionals to help her through the pregnancy. We all had her best interests in mind.

The behavior of the boy's family began to concern me to the point where I called my local police department for advice. Additionally, I called the number for an abortion

Protesters hold signs expressing regret for past abortions.

center to see how old you have to be to have an abortion in our state.

I felt safe when they told me my minor daughter had to be 16 years of age in the state of Pennsylvania to have an abortion without parental consent. I found out later that the Pennsylvania Abortion Control Act actually says that parental consent is needed for a minor under 18 years of age. It never occurred to me that I would need to check the laws of other states around me. I thought as a resident of the state of Pennsylvania that she was protected by Pennsylvania state laws. Boy, was I ever wrong.

An Unexpected Trip

On Feb. 16th [2005], I sent my daughter to her bus stop with $2.00 of lunch money. I thought she was safe at school. She and her boyfriend even had a prenatal class scheduled after school.

Chuck Asay. Reproduced by permission.

However, what really happened was that her boyfriend and his family met with her down the road from her bus stop and called a taxi. The adults put the children in the taxi to take them to the train station. His stepfather met the children at the train station, where he had to purchase my daughter's ticket since she was only fourteen. They put the children on the train from Lancaster to Philadelphia. From there, they took two subways to New Jersey. That is where his family met the children and took them to the abortion clinic, where one of the adults had made the appointment.

When my daughter started to cry and have second thoughts, they told her they would leave her in New Jersey. They planned, paid for, coerced, harassed, and threatened her into having the abortion. They left her alone during the abortion and went to eat lunch.

After the abortion, his stepfather and grandmother drove my daughter home from New Jersey and dropped her off down the road from our house.

My daughter told me that on the way home she started to cry, they got angry at her and told her there was nothing to cry about.

Anything could have happened to my daughter at the abortion facility or on the ride back home. These people did not know my daughter's medical history, yet they took her across state lines to have a medical procedure without my knowledge or consent. Our family will be responsible for the medical and psychological consequences for my daughter as a result of this procedure that was completed unbeknownst to me.

What Could Have Been Done?

I was so devastated that this could have been done that I called the local police department to see what could be done. They were just as shocked and surprised as I was that there was nothing that could be done in this horrible situation.

The state of Pennsylvania does have a parental consent law. Something has to be done to prevent this from happening to other families. This is just not acceptable to me and should not happen to families in this country. If your child goes to her school clinic for a headache, a registered nurse can't give her a Tylenol or aspirin without a parent's written permission.

As a consequence of my daughter being taken out of our state for an abortion without parental knowledge, she is suffering intense grief. My daughter cries herself to sleep at night and lives with this every day.

I think about what I could or should have done to keep her safe. Everybody tells me I did everything I could have and should have done. It doesn't make me feel any better, knowing everything I did was not enough to protect my daughter. . . .

The right of parents to protect the health and welfare of their minor daughters needs to be protected. No one should be able to circumvent state laws by performing an abortion in another state on a minor daughter without parental consent.

Analyze the essay:

1. The author uses personal testimony to help her audience see her point of view. Do you find this technique to be persuasive? Why or why not?

2. Carefully examine the way Carroll describes the family of her daughter's boyfriend. What words does she use to describe them? What details does she include about them? How does her portrayal of them affect her argument? Explain.

Parental Consent Should Not Be Required for Minors' Abortions

American Civil Liberties Union

In the following viewpoint the American Civil Liberties Union (ACLU) argues against a proposed law that would require minors to obtain parental consent before having an abortion. The ACLU explains that such a law is dangerous for girls who would face violent abuse or even death if their parents learned of their pregnancy. Teens might also resort to illegal abortions and delay getting necessary medical care if this law were passed, they warn.

The ACLU is a national organization that works to defend the rights guaranteed in the U.S. Constitution.

Consider the following questions:

1. According to the ACLU, what percentage of pregnant girls who are fourteen or younger tell their parents about their decision to have an abortion?
2. What happened to thirteen-year-old Spring Adams when her father learned that she was going to have an abortion?
3. How might parental-consent laws end up "criminalizing compassion," according to the author?

The American Civil Liberties Union opposes . . . the "Child Custody Protection Act." The bill would make

American Civil Liberties Union, "ACLU Interested Persons Memo Opposing the Teen Abandonment Act (S.851/H.R.1755), called the 'Child Custody Protection Act' by Its Sponsors," www.aclu.org, September 10, 2004. Reproduced by permission.

it a federal crime for a person, other than a parent—
including a grandmother, aunt, sibling, or clergy member—to help a teen cross state lines for an abortion unless
the teen had already fulfilled the requirements of her
home state's law restricting teens' abortions. It would
deny teenagers facing unintended pregnancies the assis-
tance of trusted adults, endanger their health, and violate their constitutional rights.

A Potential Danger for Teens

• *This legislation will not create good family communication
where it does not already exist.*

Even in the absence of any legal requirement, most young
women who are pregnant and seeking an abortion vol-
untarily involve a parent in their decision. The younger
the teenager, the more likely her parents are to know
about her decision: ninety percent of adolescents fourteen or younger report that at least one of their parents
knew of their decision. For those young women who
choose not to involve their parents, many valid reasons
compel them not to do so. For instance, one third of
teenagers who do not tell their parents about a pregnancy have already been the victims of family violence—
physical, emotional, or sexual abuse—and fear it will
recur. Long-term studies of abusive and dysfunctional
families reveal that the incidence of violence escalates
when a wife or teenage daughter becomes pregnant.
Forcing a young woman to notify her abusive parent of
a pregnancy can have dangerous, and even fatal, consequences for her and for other family members. In Idaho,
a thirteen-year-old sixth-grade student named Spring
Adams was shot to death by her father after he learned
she planned to end a pregnancy he had caused.

When a young woman determines that she cannot tell
a parent she is pregnant, a bill like this will not make her
change her mind. The same percentage of minors inform
their parents about their intent to have an abortion in
states with and without laws restricting teens' access to

abortion. This legislation will not create healthy family communication where it does not already exist. . . .

Isolating Young Women

Some teenagers must travel out of state to obtain an abortion, either because the closest abortion facility is located in a neighboring state or because there is no instate provider available at their stage of pregnancy.

The overwhelming majority of young women who obtain abortions involve an *adult* (a parent, other family member, counselor, clergy member, teacher, or adult friend) in their decision and are accompanied by someone to the health-care facility. [This bill,] however, would

Parental Consent and Notification Laws in the United States

states that require parental consent for a minor's abortion
states that require parents to be notified of a minor's abortion
states that have consent laws but are not in effect
states that have notification laws but are not in effect
states that do not have laws requiring consent or notification

* Washington, D.C., does not have laws requiring consent or notification.

Source: Planned Parenthood, "Laws Requiring Parental Consent or Notification for Minors' Abortions," www.plannedparenthood.org, July 2005.

discourage young women who are already isolated and frightened from turning to someone they trust. Knowing that anyone who helps them obtain an out-of-state abortion would risk arrest and imprisonment, many young women would be forced by this legislation to travel alone across state lines. Clearly, it is in the best interests of young women for caring, responsible adults to accompany them to an abortion provider and to escort them home after the surgery.

Drastic Acts

• *By closing outlets for teenagers facing an unwanted pregnancy, this bill would lead some to dangerous and desperate acts.* This legislation could push those teens who cannot tell a parent about a pregnancy to drastic acts that risk their health and well-being. A teenager facing an unwanted pregnancy is already in crisis. If she is unable or unwill-

Representatives of various abortion rights groups march through Atlanta in 2005 to protest restrictions on abortion access in Georgia.

ing to consult her parents, her desperation is deepened by her isolation. Teenagers in these circumstances sometimes resort to self-induced abortion or illegal abortion as a way out. These efforts all too often have tragic results. For example, Becky Bell, an Indiana teenager, died from an illegal abortion because she couldn't bear to tell her parents about her pregnancy and thus could not comply with Indiana's teen abortion law.

Out-of-state travel, in the company of a trusted companion, for a *legal* abortion, has provided many such teenagers a difficult but necessary outlet in a crisis. This bill would close that outlet, leading increasing numbers of young women to resort to the kinds of alternatives that all too often end with serious physical harm or death.

The Danger of Parental Consent Laws

Forcing teenagers to inform their parents that they are pregnant or seeking an abortion may place some at risk of violence or abuse.

Cynthia Dailard and Chinué Turner Richardson, "Teenagers' Access to Confidential Reproductive Services," *Guttmacher Report on Public Policy*, November 2005.

Deterring Compassion

• *This legislation would criminalize compassion.* This bill would impose federal criminal penalties on anyone (except a parent) who helps a young woman across state lines to obtain an abortion if she has not first complied with her home state's teen abortion law. The bill provides no exception for cases in which a young woman's health would be harmed if medical care were delayed in order for her to comply with her home state's abortion statute. The following are some examples of potential prosecutions under the bill:

> • Emergency medical personnel—both driver and technician—could be prosecuted for transporting a teen across state lines to the nearest abortion provider, even if an emergency abortion were necessary to save the young woman from serious physical harm;

• A grandmother who takes care of her granddaughter every day could be prosecuted for taking her granddaughter to another state for an abortion, even if she did not know about this federal law or was unaware of her home state's teen abortion law;

• An adult older sister could not help her teenage sister to obtain an out-of-state abortion even if both sisters were regularly subject to physical abuse by their parents and even if no local court would ever grant a petition for a court waiver.

As these examples illustrate, this legislation would criminalize caring, responsible behavior on the part of adults concerned with a young woman's well-being. It would deter trustworthy adults and professionals from helping a young woman to obtain an out-of-state abortion no matter what the circumstances. It thus would create a barrier to safe, timely medical care and would endanger young women's well-being.

Analyze the essay:

1. Do you think that minors should be allowed to have an abortion without their parents' consent? Why or why not?

2. The American Civil Liberties Union is a well-known political organization that openly supports the right of women to have an abortion. Does this information influence your assessment of their argument? Explain.

It Is Acceptable to Abort a Fetus with Severe Disabilities

Maria Eftimiades

In the following essay Maria Eftimiades explains why she believes that terminating a pregnancy is acceptable if the fetus has severe disabilities. She relates her own experience of carrying a fetus that turned out to have Down syndrome, an abnormality that can result in serious mental and physical handicaps. Eftimiades and her boyfriend decided it would be wrong for them to bear a child who would likely have a very difficult life. The author notes that this experience helped her realize how private the abortion decision is. She concludes it is unfair to judge women who are faced with this difficult choice.

Eftimiades is a national correspondent for *People* magazine.

Consider the following questions:

1. How old was Eftimiades when she became pregnant? What are the chances that a woman her age will have a Down syndrome baby?
2. Why did the author's mother want her to tell friends and family that she had had a miscarriage?
3. How did the hospital staff treat Eftimiades when she went to have her abortion?

"So when do you go for the abortion?" my friend asked, her voice sympathetic.

Maria Eftimiades, "One Woman's Choice," *The Washington Post*, November 15, 2005. Reproduced by permission of the author.

"Wednesday," I replied, and then hurriedly got off the phone. I called Mike, my boyfriend, in tears, complaining about how inconsiderate people are, how no one thinks before they speak. The truth was, until I heard the word "abortion," it hadn't occurred to me that I was actually having one.

I was, of course. But we'd been using euphemisms for days, ever since my doctor called to say my amniocentesis results "weren't good." We'd say "when we go to the hospital" or "the appointment" or "after the procedure, we can try again."

Bad News

We were driving to the post office, Mike and I, near our home when my cell phone rang and I recognized the OB-GYN's number. I said, "It's the doctor," and then, a little later, "Oh, no." Mike pulled over and held my hand while I listened. It didn't take long; the doctor didn't have much to say. He suggested we digest the news and call him later.

When I hung up, I told Mike, "It's Down syndrome" and we went home and lay in bed for the rest of the day. We were shocked.

Perhaps we shouldn't have been. I was a few weeks from my 42nd birthday. Mike was 52. This was to be the first child for both of us. We'd read the statistics: at my age, a 1-in-100 chance of a Down syndrome baby, although my doctor said later he'd put the figure closer to 1-in-40. Not the best odds, but somehow we never expected we'd be the couple to receive bad news. . . .

Trying to Be Careful

From the start of my pregnancy, I tried to be so careful. Mike brought home fresh fruit for me every evening, and I fretted when the pharmacy didn't have my prenatal vitamins in stock and I had to wait an extra day. I even wrote to Starbucks to request they add black decaffeinated tea to their menu. (Herbals aren't good for pregnant women.)

Down Syndrome: Risk by Age of Mother	
Mother's Age	**Risk Factor of Down Syndrome**
15 years	1/1,663 births
20 years	1/1,627 births
25 years	1/1,487 births
30 years	1/1,089 births
35 years	1/509 births
40 years	1/156 births
45 years	1/40 births
49 years	1/12 births

Source: Donald Urquhart, "Down Syndrome Risk by Age of Mother," www.cdadc.com /ds/downsyndromepregnancysymptoms.htm, 2005.

Though we tried not to get too excited, Mike and I began searching for names—we even found ourselves studying the credits at the end of movies. For a girl, we were far apart; for a boy, we leaned toward John—we both have a brother with that name.

Once I had the amnio and saw from the sonogram it was a boy, I thought I was in the clear: It didn't occur to me to wait for the test results before sharing the news more freely. One Sunday morning I told my softball friends I was pregnant and they cheered the prospect of a new player and told me I'd done the team well by producing a boy. The very next weekend, I stayed home from the game, devastated by my whirling misfortune.

Later, one of my teammates suggested that I tell others I had a miscarriage.

"You never know how people will react," he said.

My mother, too, was a proponent of the miscarriage story. She told two of my brothers the truth, she told the third that I'd suddenly lost the baby. That brother's wife was a Catholic, and my mother was taking no chances.

"People are funny," she said.

Making the Choice

I've heard the abortion debate my whole life, and while I was a newspaper reporter I had covered stories about clinic bombings and protests. I interviewed Randall Terry of Operation Rescue when I was in my twenties. I talked with his supporters who stood outside clinics and imitated babies crying, begging "Mommy, don't kill me," when abortion-seekers passed by.

Emotions run high as abortion rights activists respond to a march by antiabortionists in San Francisco in 2006.

Once I became one of those women ending a pregnancy, I found myself wondering how I'd react under that kind of pressure. I remember a cop I interviewed once telling me about a "good rape," one where the attacker was a stranger and there was no ambiguity, no chance of blaming the victim because she had drunk too much or invited her date in for coffee. I wonder if it's the same for abortion. If your child will be born with a severe disability, is there a "Get Out of Jail Free" card or are you still a baby killer?

While I have no doubt there can be joys and victories in raising a mentally handicapped child, for me and for Mike, it's a painful journey that we believe is better not taken. To know now that our son would be retarded, perhaps profoundly, gives us the choice of not continuing the pregnancy. We don't want a life like that for our child, and the added worry that we wouldn't be around long enough to care for him throughout his life. . . .

One night, a few days after we learned of the diagnosis, I dreamed that I saw our baby. . . . In the dream, we were in a bookstore, the three of us. I heard gunfire. Then, the baby crawled away. I woke up missing him, mourning the child we wouldn't have.

A Personal Decision

I'm sure pro-lifers don't give you the right to grieve for the baby you chose not to bring into the world (another euphemism, although avoiding the word "abortion" doesn't take any sting out of the decision to have one). Only now do I understand how entirely personal the decision to terminate a pregnancy is and how wrong it feels to bring someone else's morality into the discussion.

I was lucky. When I walked into the hospital, no one knew why, or cared. The nurses were kind and the doctor held my hand as the anesthesia took over.

As for that baby that will never be, I will remember him always. But I'm quite certain that I made the right choice for the three of us.

Analyze the essay:

1. Do you agree with the author that it is better to abort a fetus that would be born with severe disabilities? Why or why not?
2. Toward the end of her essay Eftimiades recounts a dream she had after she learned about the Down syndrome diagnosis. Why does she include this? Do you think that it makes her argument more convincing? Explain.

It Is Wrong to Abort a Fetus with Severe Disabilities

Lori Scheck

Lori Scheck is the mother of a son with Down syndrome. In the following selection she argues that it is wrong to abort a fetus that has birth defects. In her opinion it is immoral to deny a child life just because it will be born with challenging disabilities. Doing so suggests that disabled people—and others who do not "measure up" to certain standards—are better off not being alive. Scheck maintains that raising her disabled son has brought her family both joys and frustrations, just as her nondisabled children did. Allowing disabled children to be born is the only right choice to make, she concludes.

Consider the following questions:

1. Why did Scheck refuse to have a test to detect the presence of birth defects?
2. What does the author say that her family learned from having a child with Down syndrome?
3. What does Scheck compare abortion to in the final paragraph?

The morning is as hectic as ever. I am scrambling eggs and warming one of last night's dinner rolls for my son's breakfast. He is getting his shoes and socks on. It isn't easy because he would rather be playing his video

Lori Scheck, "A Normal Life," www.cwfa.org, Concerned Women for America, November 23, 2005. Reproduced by permission.

A girl who has Down Syndrome enjoys looking at a book with her father.

game. We have to be ready for school early this morning so we can review words for his spelling test one last time. After I help him clean his glasses (because he has a much higher tolerance level for smudge than I do) and comb his hair (because I happen to believe that a part should actually look like a straight line) he grabs his backpack, his snack and his water bottle, and rushes out to catch the school bus. My son is Stephen. He is 13 years old, he attends a local middle school and he has Down syndrome.

More Normal than Special

Stephen is the last of my husband's and my four children, the first three being what we would consider "normal." Having gone through the infant, toddler, elementary and middle school stages with our first three children, we had a pretty good idea of what they entail. What we experienced with our special needs child was very much the same as the first three. We laughed at his first smile and first giggles. He crawled like a GI Joe Army man for the longest time. We celebrated his first steps, first words, and first day in preschool. Yes, we had to wait longer for those accomplishments to come to pass, but they all did. In fact, the waiting made the accomplishment cause for greater celebration than with the first three kids. We learned to enjoy every little thing in his life. Our life with Stephen has been much more normal than it has been "special."

I was 33 when Stephen was born, not yet the age where a mom is considered high risk for giving birth to a child with Down syndrome. Because I had enjoyed three healthy, successful pregnancies before, I had no doubt that this one would be the same. Thirteen years ago the AFP blood test, which is given early in the second trimester to try to discern the presence of birth defects, was fairly new and I did not know a lot about it. When offered the test I refused as I knew that, regardless of the outcome, I would continue the pregnancy and bring this child into the world. It wasn't until after Stephen was born that the suggestion that our new baby had a disability was even presented to my husband and me. I was glad to have it that way. It removed pre-birth anxiety from my experience. It also allowed me to cope with the diagnosis as I cradled a beautiful baby in my arms . . . much easier than trying to cradle a test result and sonogram picture.

Who Is Worth Bringing into the World?

Our family has learned much from having Stephen in our world. Not only did we learn various terminologies and developmental strategies, we learned a lot about ourselves. If our kids are smart or beautiful, athletic or talented in some way, we tend to feel this enormous sense of pride—as though we had anything at all to do with them having those characteristics. The converse is true as well. If they are retarded or handicapped or in some way don't measure up to the standard of our culture, then we feel embarrassment or shame. Both thoughts are ridiculous. Our children's talents, abilities or disabilities are gifts from God. We have no control over such things. We do, however, have control over our attitude and response to these circumstances.

Our culture has created an environment where it's okay to abort a child if he or she, for some reason, will not "measure up," or will be hard to care for. Who sets the standard for whether or not someone is worth bringing into the world? I'll be the first to tell you that special needs children are not the only ones who are hard work and sometimes bring frustration. My older children have done their fair share of that as well. All children, normal, handicapped, able and disabled, can be a source of joy and pride as well as heartache and frustration.

Pro-life supporters demonstrate in California. Beliefs on the abortion issue are highly personal and often impassioned.

No Guarantees

The medical profession is not a fortune teller. It cannot guarantee a child's future outcome. Doctors may be able to tell you about the baby's genetic code, but they cannot determine his character or happiness quotient. I wonder

if the parents of young people who shoot their classmates at school would have chosen abortion if they could have known about their child's outcome in advance. That's part of the adventure of parenting. There are no guarantees.

When I hear about people who have aborted such a child because they didn't want him to have to "live a life like that," I am incredulous. How someone comes to the conclusion that not allowing a child to live at all is somehow better than living as a special needs child is beyond comprehension. Aborting a disabled child removes the option of looking at the glass as half empty or half full. Abortion takes the glass and heaves it over the side of a cliff while the pieces shatter on the rocks below. While it may eliminate the disappointment, sorrow and frustration, it also eliminates the hope, joy and pride of accomplishment that a child can bring. What a travesty. What arrogance. What right do we have to destroy that little person because he doesn't measure up to someone's standard? If the choice were left up to the child, I am confident he or she would choose life. I know my son would.

Analyze the essay:
1. Scheck begins her essay with a descriptive anecdote about her son with Down syndrome. Why do you think she introduces her argument this way?
2. In this viewpoint the author argues against aborting fetuses with birth defects. In the previous viewpoint the author maintains that such abortions may be necessary. After reading both of these viewpoints, what is your opinion on these kinds of abortions? Explain your reasoning.

Section Two:
Model Essays
and Writing
Exercises

The Five-Paragraph Essay

An essay is a short piece of writing that discusses or analyzes one topic. The five-paragraph essay is a form commonly used in school assignments and tests. Every five-paragraph essay begins with an introduction, ends with a conclusion, and features three supporting paragraphs in the middle.

The Thesis Statement. The introduction includes the essay's thesis statement. The thesis statement presents the argument or point the author is trying to make about the topic. The essays in this book all have different thesis statements because they are making different arguments about abortion.

The thesis statement should clearly tell the reader what the essay will be about. A focused thesis statement helps determine what will be in the essay; the subsequent paragraphs are spent developing and supporting its argument.

The Introduction. In addition to presenting the thesis statement, a well-written introductory paragraph captures the attention of the reader and explains why the topic being explored is important. It may provide the reader with background information on the subject matter or feature an anecdote that illustrates a point relevant to the topic. It could also present startling information that clarifies the point of the essay or puts forth a contradictory position that the essay will refute. Further techniques for writing an introduction are found later in this section.

The Supporting Paragraphs. The introduction is followed by three (or more) supporting paragraphs. These are the main body of the essay. Each paragraph presents and develops a subtopic that supports the essay's thesis statement. Each subtopic is then supported with its own facts, details, and examples. The writer can use various kinds of supporting material and details to back up the topic of each supporting paragraph. These may include statistics, quotations from people with special knowledge or expertise, historic facts, and anecdotes. A rule of writing is that specific and concrete examples are more convincing than vague, general, or unsupported assertions.

The Conclusion. The conclusion is the paragraph that closes the essay. Its function is to summarize or reiterate the main idea of the essay. It may recall an idea from the introduction or briefly examine the larger implications of the thesis. Because the conclusion is also the last chance a writer has to make an impression on the reader, it is important that it not simply repeat what has been presented elsewhere in the essay but close it in a clear, final, and memorable way.

Although the order of the essay's component paragraphs is important, they do not have to be written in that order. Some writers like to decide on a thesis and write the introductory paragraph first. Other writers like to focus first on the body of the essay and write the introduction and conclusion later.

Pitfalls to Avoid

When writing essays about controversial issues such as abortion, it is important to remember that disputes over the material are common precisely because there are many different perspectives. Remember to state your arguments in careful and measured terms. Evaluate your topic fairly—avoid overstating negative qualities of one perspective or understating positive qualities of another. Use examples, facts, and details to support any assertions you make.

The Persuasive Essay

There are many types of essays, but in general they are usually short compositions in which the writer expresses and discusses an opinion about something. In the persuasive essay the writer tries to persuade (convince) the reader to do something or to agree with the writer's opinion about something. Examples of persuasive writing are easy to find. Advertising is one common example. Through commercial and print ads, companies try to convince the public to buy their products for specific reasons. Much everyday writing is persuasive, too. Letters to the editor, posts from sports fans on team Web sites, even handwritten notes urging a friend to listen to a new CD—all are examples of persuasive writing.

The Tools of Persuasion

The writer of the persuasive essay uses various tools to persuade the reader. Here are some of them:

• **Facts and statistics.** A fact is a statement that no one, typically, would disagree with. It can be verified by information in reputable resources, such as encyclopedias, almanacs, government Web sites, or reference books about the topic of the fact.

It is important to note that facts and statistics can be misstated (written down or quoted incorrectly), misinterpreted (not understood correctly by the user), or misused (not used fairly). But if a writer uses facts and statistics properly, they can add authority to the writer's essay.

• **Opinions.** An opinion is what a person thinks about something. It can be contested or argued with. However, opinions of people who are experts on the topic or who have personal experience are often very convincing. Many

Examples of Facts and Statistics

Americans celebrate their nation's birth every fourth of July.

Sacramento is the capital of California.

The average American eats 252 eggs each year.

A 2005 survey by the Science Museum in London found that one in fifteen people have reported seeing a UFO.

persuasive essays are written to convince the reader that the writer's opinion is worth believing and acting on.

- **Testimonials.** A testimonial is a statement given by a person who is thought to be an expert or who has another trait people admire, such as being a celebrity. Television commercials frequently use testimonials to convince watchers to buy the products they are advertising.

- **Examples and anecdotes.** An example is something that is representative of a group or type ("red" is an example of the group "color"). Examples are used to help define, describe, or illustrate something to make it more understandable. Anecdotes are extended examples. They are little stories with a beginning, middle, and end. They can be used just like examples to explain something or to show something about a topic.

- **Appeals to reason.** One way to convince readers that an opinion or action is right is to appeal to reason or logic. This often involves the idea that if some ideas are true, another must also be true. Here is an example of one type of appeal to reason:

    Access to abortion is protected by the Ninth Amendment's explanation of an individual's right to privacy. If you support the freedoms guaranteed by the U.S. Constitution, you should support a woman's right to choose abortion.

- **Appeals to emotion.** Another way to persuade readers to believe or do something is to appeal to their emotions—love, fear, pity, loyalty, and anger are some of the emotions to which writers appeal. A writer who wants to persuade the reader that abortion is wrong might appeal to the reader's sense of love ("If you cherish innocent babies, you should do everything in your power to outlaw abortion.")

•**Ridicule and name-calling.** Ridicule and name-calling are not good techniques to use in a persuasive essay. Instead of exploring the strengths of the topic, the writer who uses these relies on making those who oppose the main idea look foolish, evil, or stupid. In most cases the writer who does this weakens the argument.

• **Bandwagon.** The writer who uses the bandwagon technique uses the idea that "Everybody thinks this or is doing this; therefore it is valid." The bandwagon method is not a very authoritative way to convince your reader of your point.

Words and Phrases Common to Persuasive Essays

accordingly	it seems clear that
because	it stands to reason
consequently	it then follows that
clearly	obviously
for this reason	since
this is why	subsequently
indeed	therefore
it is necessary to	thus
it makes sense to	we must

Partial-Birth Abortions Should Be Banned

Editor's Notes The following essay takes a stance against a form of late-term abortion that is usually performed when the mother is five or six months pregnant. The phrase partial-birth abortion is commonly used by those who oppose the procedure. Believing it to be a form of infanticide, many antiabortionists emphasize that this surgery destroys fetuses that are significantly developed.

This essay takes the stance that partial-birth abortion is cruel and inhumane. It discusses three supporting ideas: that the surgery is a painful form of killing, that it is unnecessary and dangerous for the mother, and that it undermines public trust in the medical profession. The essay then concludes with a summary of the main points and a call to action.

As you read, pay attention to the way the essay is organized. The sidebar notes provide additional information and commentary. Also note that all sources are cited using MLA style. For more information on how to cite your sources, see Appendix C.

Refers to thesis and topic sentences

Refers to supporting details

The essay begins with an imaginary scene intended to provoke an emotional reaction.

Paragraph 1

Imagine being immobile in a dark, warm space. Without warning, you are stabbed in the back of the head. You jerk in shock with the pain. As the contents of your skull are sucked out through the stab wound, your life quickly drains away. Does this sound like a nightmare? Or a horror movie? Unfortunately, it is not. This gruesome scene is an all-too-brutal reality for at least two thousand innocent human beings each year in the United States. This procedure, known as partial-birth abortion, is a form of infanticide that should be illegal in any society that views itself as humane.

The final sentence is the thesis of the essay.

Performed on fetuses that are five or six months old, this disturbing operation is dubbed "partial-birth" abortion because a physician begins by inducing labor. First, the doctor delivers everything but the infant's head from the uterus. Then he or she uses scissors to cut a hole in the base of the baby's skull so that its brain can be removed. The empty skull then collapses, enabling the baby's dying body to pass more easily through the birth canal. Brain surgeon Robert J. White states that "partial-birth abortion—with its tissue compression, its pulling of limbs and body, its anatomical distortion—must be an extremely painful experience for the fetus as it [advances] through the birth canal" (White 4). The surgical procedure is even more excruciating, says White, because unborn infants are even more sensitive to pain than newborns or older children are. During a partial-birth abortion, a baby feels intense pain when its skull is pierced and its brain is sucked out. The fact that this operation is essentially the torturous killing of a premature infant should ban it outright.

> The graphic description starting with the second sentence, as well as the use of "baby" (rather than "fetus") is another appeal to emotion.

> The author quotes an expert to help support the paragraph's main point.

> The final sentence is the topic sentence of paragraph 2.

Some people maintain that a partial-birth abortion is necessary when a woman's health is threatened by her pregnancy or when the fetus has serious physical defects. However, the sad truth is that most of these abortions are performed on healthy mothers and healthy fetuses. According to Illinois physician Mark Neerhoff, 56 percent of partial-birth abortions are done as a result of fetal disabilities, some of them as minor as a cleft lip (Neerhoff 13). So far, no studies have shown that partial-birth abortions are required to protect a woman's life. The procedure can actually endanger the mother's health in several ways. A woman undergoing a partial-birth abortion risks accidental cuts and severe bleeding when the doctor blindly stabs at the unborn child's skull. This complication can lead to hemorrhage, shock, and death. In addition, women who have undergone these abortions are more likely to have miscarriages and other health-endangering

> The author brings in an opposing view in order to debunk it.

> How do these statistics support the thesis of the essay?

complications in future pregnancies. Apparently, partial-birth abortion benefits neither babies nor mothers.

The topic sentence ends the paragraph.

Paragraph 4

While its harms are obvious, the effects of partial-birth abortion extend beyond the small number of people who undergo this procedure. Physicians, who have taken an oath to protect life and to do no harm, are actually expected to destroy a partly born child during this operation. Partial-birth abortion conflicts with the goals of the medical profession and undermines the public's trust in doctors, nurses, and others who have vowed to safeguard health. The continuing legality of this procedure makes it seem as if the medical profession has little respect for life. Do we want to live in a society that allows its healers to be killers? What kind of values does that help to instill?

Here the topic sentence also provides a transition into the fourth paragraph.

The author uses rhetorical questions—questions that require no answer—for persuasive effect.

Paragraph 5

Partial-birth abortion is a brutal and inhumane procedure that destroys the life of a partly born infant. It also endangers women's health and starkly contradicts the aims of the healing professions. A society that fails to stop partial-birth abortion is a society that is blind to the humanity of infants and all other vulnerable forms of life. Those who wish to preserve a civilized society must act now to ban this cruel procedure.

The author concludes by summarizing the main points and issuing a call to action.

Works Cited

Neerhoff, Mark. Qtd. in Introduction. *Abortion: Opposing Viewpoints*. Ed. Mary E. Williams. San Diego: Greenhaven, 2003: 13.

White, Robert J. "Partial-Birth Abortion: A Neurosurgeon Speaks." *America* 18 Oct. 1997: 4.

Exercise A: Create an Outline from an Existing Essay

It often helps to create an outline of the five-paragraph essay before you write it. The outline can help you organize the information, arguments, quotes, and evidence you have gathered in your research.

For this exercise, create an outline that could have been used to write the first model essay. This "reverse engineering" exercise is meant to help you become familiar with using outlines to classify and arrange information. Part of the outline has already been started. Fill in the rest.

Outline for Essay One: "Partial-Birth Abortions Should Be Banned"

Thesis statement: Partial-birth abortion is a form of infanticide that should be banned.

I. Introduction: Partial-birth abortion is a horrific surgery.

   A. It involves stabbing infants in the back of the head.
   B. It is performed on at least two thousand fetuses a year in the United States.

II. Supporting paragraph 1, topic sentence: This operation is the torturous killing of a premature infant.

   A. First evidence: It is performed on five- or six-month-old fetuses.
   B. Second evidence:
   C. Third evidence: Brain surgeon Robert J. White says that this procedure causes extreme pain.
      1. It compresses tissue and pulls on the fetus's limbs and body.
      2.

III. Supporting paragraph 2, topic sentence: Partial-birth abortion benefits neither babies nor mothers.

A. First evidence: Most are performed on healthy mothers with healthy fetuses.

B. Second evidence:

C. Third evidence:

IV. Supporting paragraph 3, topic sentence:

A. First evidence:

B. Second evidence:

C. Third evidence:

V. Conclusion, topic sentence:

Access to Abortion Benefits Women

Editor's Notes The following essay uses a variety of persuasive techniques to convince the reader that access to abortion benefits women. As with the previous five-paragraph essay, its thesis statement is in the introductory paragraph, and the three supporting paragraphs all have a topic sentence as well as supporting details that support the thesis. As you read, observe how the essay is organized and which persuasive tools are used. In addition, take note of how certain word choices, such as "antichoice," (rather than pro-life or antiabortion) affect the tone of the essay.

▪ Refers to thesis and topic sentences

▫ Refers to supporting details

Paragraph 1

Antichoice advocates often claim that abortion not only kills babies, but that it also harms women. They insist that having an abortion increases the risk of breast cancer, sterility, future pregnancy complications, and mental health problems. They also contend that women who have abortions are suppressing their nurturing instincts because they are selfish or irresponsible. These arguments, however, are really an empty propaganda campaign against reproductive choice. The truth is that access to safe and legal abortion has had a positive impact on women's health and women's lives.

The writer begins by summarizing the arguments of opponents and then expressing disagreement.

What is the essay's thesis?

Paragraph 2

Legal access to abortion in the United States has saved women's lives. According to the National Abortion and Reproductive Rights League (NARAL), before the 1973 legalization of abortion, more than five thousand women likely died each year as a direct result of criminal "back alley" abortions. Many of these deaths were caused by inexperienced surgeons operating under unsanitary conditions. Between 1973 and 1997, however, the death rate

What is the topic sentence for paragraph 2?

By including numbers and statistics, the author appeals to reason and logic.

What sentences in paragraph 2 express an opinion?

What is the topic sentence of paragraph 3?

How does this anecdote support the paragraph's topic sentence?

Which sentences are expressions of fact? Which are expressions of opinion?

per 100,000 legal abortion procedures decreased from 4.1 to 0.6 (NARAL). Pregnancy itself carries substantial risks—women who have a full-term pregnancy have a death rate ten times higher than those who have abortions. Given these facts, it is frustrating that opponents of abortion seem solely concerned with the fetus's life while ignoring the life and health of the mother. Surely her life and health deserve consideration too.

Paragraph 3

A woman's life and health deserve consideration even in the case of abortions that occur past the first trimester. The late-term dilation and extraction procedure, referred to as "partial-birth abortion" by its opponents, is the least common form of abortion—but it can be lifesaving. Critics claim that it is a form of infanticide because it is performed on women who are more than five months pregnant. But Coreen Costello's story sheds a different light on the need for this procedure. In April 1995, when Coreen was seven months pregnant, doctors discovered that her fetus had a terminal neuromuscular disease. The fetus's body had stiffened and became wedged in an odd position. In addition, fluid had built up to dangerous levels in Coreen's uterus. Several experts agreed that a dilation and extraction procedure was necessary to prevent additional life-threatening complications. Coreen weathered the surgery well and her health was restored. The following year she became pregnant again and gave birth to a healthy son.

Paragraph 4

Contrary to antichoice arguments, most women who have abortions take motherhood seriously. When a woman seeks an abortion, it is often because she recognizes that she would be unable to responsibly fulfill a parental role at that point in her life. Indeed, many women have important relationship, financial, and educational constraints that they take into account when considering parenthood. According to reproductive health researcher Felicia H.

Stewart and obstetrician Philip D. Darney, "Women typically approach the decision [to have an abortion] with careful thought, and for many women (and couples), the moral importance of being the best parents they can be is a significant issue" (Stewart 38). Thus, legalized abortion actually promotes responsible motherhood by allowing women the choice of when to reproduce.

Paragraph 5

Access to safe and legal abortion is a boon, not a blight, for women. Such access enhances a woman's life and health by ensuring that she can safely terminate a pregnancy if need be. Those who support legalized abortion are endorsing a woman's right to make important moral choices and to determine the direction of her life. If we believe that women are responsible for these choices, we must fight to keep abortion safe and legal.

Where is the topic sentence in this paragraph?

How does the writer avoid simply restating the thesis?

Works Cited

NARAL Pro-Choice America. "*Roe v. Wade* and the Right to Choose." 1 Jan. 2004 < http://www.prochoiceamer ica.org > .

Stewart, Felicia H., and Philip D. Darney. "Abortion: Teaching Why as Well as How." *Perspectives on Sexual and Reproductive Health*. Jan.–Feb. 2003: 37–39.

Exercise A: Identifying Persuasive Techniques

Essayists use many techniques to persuade you to agree with their ideas or to do something they want you to do. Some of the most common techniques are described in Preface B of this section, "The Persuasive Essay." These techniques are facts and statistics, opinions, testimonials, examples and anecdotes, appeals to reason, appeals to emotion, ridicule and name-calling, and bandwagon. Go back to Preface B and review these techniques. Remember that most of them can be used to enhance your essay, but some of them—particularly ridiculing, name-calling, and bandwagon—can detract from the essay's effectiveness. Nevertheless, you should be able to recognize them in the essays you read.

Some writers use one persuasive technique throughout their whole essay. For example, the essay may be one extended anecdote, or the writer may rely entirely on statistics. But most writers typically use a combination of persuasive techniques. Model Essay Two does this. The sidebar notes point out some of the persuasive techniques used in the essay.

Read Essay Two again and see if you can find every persuasive technique used. Put that information in the following table. Part of the table is filled in for you. Explanatory notes are underneath the table. (**NOTE: You will not fill in every box. No paragraph contains all of the techniques.**)

	Paragraph 1 Sentence #	Paragraph 2 Sentence #	Paragraph 3 Sentence #	Paragraph 4 Sentence #	Paragraph 5 Sentence #
Fact	1 (note 1)	1, 6 (note 4)			
Statistic		2, 4, 5 (note 5)			
Opinion	4, 5 (note 3)	3, 7 (note 6)			
Testimonial					
Example	2, 3 (note 2)				
Anecdote					
Appeal to Reason					
Appeal to Emotion		3 (note 6) 8 (note 7)			
Ridicule					
Name-Calling					
Bandwagon					

NOTES

1. Sentence one is a statement of fact that can be corroborated by reading the arguments of those who oppose abortion.

2. Sentences two and three are each examples of the arguments of abortion opponents.

3. Sentence four is an opinion. Many may not agree that the statements of abortion opponents are an empty propaganda campaign. Sentence five is also an opinion, because others may have evidence that they believe shows that abortion has had a negative impact on women's lives.

4. Sentence one of the second paragraph is a statement of fact that is supported by the information given in sentence two. Sentence six is a factual statement, a form of general knowledge.

5. Statistics: Sentence two—five thousand American women a year died before abortion was legalized; sentence four—the death rate decreased from 4.1 to 0.6 per 100,000 abortions; sentence five—women who give birth have a death rate ten times higher than do women who have abortions.

6. Sentence three is an opinion—the word "probably" signals that it may not be true. This is also an appeal to emotion. Sentence seven is an opinion also, because opponents to abortion may disagree that they ignore the life and health of the woman.

7. Sentence eight is an appeal to emotion, inviting the reader to see access to abortion as a way to protect the lives and health of women.

Now, look at the table you have produced. Which persuasive techniques does this essay rely on most heavily? Which are not used at all?

Look back at Essay One. See if you can find any of the missing persuasive techniques in that essay. As you read Essay Three, watch for the persuasive techniques it contains.

The Right to Privacy Ensures Access to Abortions

Editor's Notes The following essay has more than five paragraphs, but it follows the same basic pattern as a five-paragraph essay. You can use this pattern for an essay of any length.

This essay was written to convince the reader that the right to have an abortion, while not directly expressed in the Constitution, is protected under constitutional freedoms outlined in the Ninth and Fourteenth Amendments. The writer argues that reproductive choice, which includes the right to give birth and the right to have an abortion, is necessary in a pluralistic society.

Refers to thesis and topic sentences

Refers to supporting details

Paragraph 1

Do women in the United States have the legal right to choose abortion? Most Americans would answer yes to this question, but that is not exactly the case. It is more accurate to say that individuals have the right to privacy, which includes a woman's right to decide whether to become a mother. Recognizing that access to abortion is a privacy-rights issue is important if we want it to remain safe and legal.

What kind of audience does the writer presume will be reading this essay?

What is the essay's thesis?

Paragraph 2

Abortion became legal in America in 1973, when the Supreme Court heard the landmark case known as *Roe versus Wade*. Examining the case sheds light on the connection between privacy and reproductive choice. The case began in 1969, when a young divorced woman named Norma McCorvey found herself with an unwanted pregnancy. Out of work and with no reliable income, McCorvey needed to end the pregnancy. But abortion was illegal in her home state of Texas except when the pregnancy

Why does the author include these details about Norma McCorvey?

endangered the woman's life. Although she was unable to obtain an abortion, she did find two attorneys, Linda Coffee and Sarah Weddington, who wanted to challenge antiabortion laws. With the pseudonym "Jane Roe," she agreed to represent all women who had been denied abortions in a lawsuit against Texas district attorney Henry Wade.

Paragraph 3

What is the topic sentence in paragraph 3?

Attorneys Coffee and Weddington argued that the Texas antiabortion law violated the Fourteenth and Ninth Amendments to the U.S. Constitution. The "due process" clause of the Fourteenth Amendment says that states cannot deny an individual's right to life, liberty, or property. The crux of the attorneys' argument, however, rested on the Ninth Amendment. This amendment ensures certain rights that are not specifically outlined in the Constitution, including the right to privacy. An individual's right to privacy includes a woman's right to decide whether to give birth, Coffee and Weddington argued.

How do these specific details about the trial support the essay's thesis?

Paragraph 4

The lawyers representing Wade, on the other hand, claimed that the unborn child's right to life is protected by the Fourteenth Amendment. In effect, they argued that the rights of the fetus outweigh a woman's right to privacy. Roe's lawyers countered that "life is an ongoing process. It is almost impossible to define a point at which life begins or perhaps even at which life ends." Since there has been no consensus on when life actually begins, they argued, the fetus should not be seen as a person with the same rights as the already born. The majority opinion in *Roe v. Wade* concurred with this argument. In doing so, they declared that the word "person" in the Constitution, and therefore the Fourteenth Amendment, does not include the unborn.

Notice that the writer clarifies why the Fourteenth Amendment does not apply to fetuses.

Paragraph 5

These Supreme Court clarifications are important. In essence, the justices agreed that the decision to abort or to give birth is a woman's private choice. It is the decision that makes the most sense in a culture like ours, in which people hold a wide variety of opinions on the morality of abortion. This means, for example, that women who have traditional religious beliefs have the right to reject abortion for themselves because they believe it is wrong. Freedom of speech also grants them the right to try to persuade others that abortion is wrong. But nothing in the Constitution gives them the right to force their personal beliefs on others by outlawing abortion. Such a ban would violate the individual's right to privacy.

> Why do you think the writer uses the example of someone who opposes abortion?

Paragraph 6

Ultimately, culture, personal beliefs, and the input of loved ones and medical experts should be the only factors weighing on a woman's reproductive choices. It is not the place of government, lawmakers, or judges to be making such life-altering decisions for women. All that government should do is support a woman's choice to have, or not to have, a child. And the best way for the government to do this is to respect individual privacy and keep abortion legal.

> What is the topic sentence of the final paragraph?

> Examine this final paragraph carefully. What persuasive techniques are used to convince you of its point of view?

Works Cited

Roe v. Wade. No. 70-18. Supreme Ct. of the US. 22 Jan. 1973.

Exercise A: Writing Introductions and Conclusions

The introductory and concluding paragraphs can greatly improve your essay by quickly imparting to your reader the essay's main idea. Well-written introductions not only present the essay's thesis statement, but also grab the attention of the reader and tell why the topic being explored is important and interesting. The conclusion reiterates the thesis statement, but also is the last chance for the writer to make an impression on the reader and to drive home his/her main points.

The Introduction

There are several techniques you can use in the opening paragraph to attract the reader's attention. An essay can start with

- an anecdote: a brief story that illustrates a point relevant to the topic;
- startling information: true and pertinent facts or statistics that illustrate the point of the essay—a brief opening assertion that can then be elaborated upon over the next few sentences;
- setting up and knocking down a position: an assertion proponents of one side of a controversy believe, followed by statements that challenge that assertion;
- summary information: general introductory information about the topic, followed by gradually more specific statements that lead into the thesis statement at the end of the paragraph.

Reread the introductory paragraphs of the model essays and of the six viewpoints in Section One. Identify which of the techniques described above are used in these essays. How else do they get the attention of the reader while presenting the thesis statement of the essay?

The Conclusion

The conclusion brings the essay to a close by summarizing or restating its main argument(s). Good conclusions go beyond simply repeating the argument, however. They also answer the reader's question of "so what?"—in other words, they tell why the argument is important to consider. Some conclusions may also explore the broader implications of the thesis argument. They may close with a quotation or refer back to an anecdote or event in the essay. In essays over controversial topics, such as abortion, the conclusion should reiterate which side the essay is taking.

1. Reread the concluding paragraphs of the model essays and of the six viewpoints in the previous section. Which were most effective in driving their arguments home to the reader? What sorts of devices did they use?

2. Take the concluding paragraph from one of the essays in this book. Cross out the restated thesis; cross out the summing-up of the essay's main points. What is left? What has the writer done as a last effort to persuade the reader?

As you prepare to write your own persuasive essay, think about the analysis you have done for this exercise. This may help you compose your own effective introduction and conclusion.

Write Your Own Persuasive Five-Paragraph Essay

Using the information from this book, write your own five-paragraph persuasive essay on a topic related to abortion. The following steps are suggestions on how to get started.

Step One: Choose your topic.
Think carefully before deciding what topic to write your persuasive essay on. Is there any subject that particularly fascinates you? Is there an issue you strongly support, or feel strongly against? Is there a topic you would like to learn more about? Ask yourself such questions before selecting your essay topic. Refer to Appendix D: Sample Essay Topics if you need help selecting a topic.

Step Two: Write down questions and answers about the topic.
Before you begin writing, you will need to think carefully about what ideas your essay will contain. This is a process known as brainstorming. Brainstorming involves asking yourself questions and coming up with ideas to discuss in your essay. Possible questions that will help you with the brainstorming process include:

- Why is this topic important?
- Why should people be interested in this topic?
- How can I make this essay interesting to the reader?
- What question am I going to address in this paragraph or essay?
- What facts, ideas, or quotes can I use to support the answer to my question?
- Will the question's answer reveal a preference for one subject over another?

Step Three: Gather facts and ideas related to your topic.
This book contains several places to find information, including the viewpoints and the appendixes. In addition, you may want to research the books, articles, and Web sites listed in Section Three or do additional research in your local library.

Step Four: Develop a workable thesis statement.

Use what you have written down in steps two and three to help you articulate the main point or argument you want to make in your essay. It should be expressed in a clear sentence and make an arguable or supportable point.

Examples:

Late-Term Abortions Should Remain Legal
(This could be the thesis statement of a persuasive essay that uses statistics, testimony, or anecdotes to convince the reader.)

Women Experience Health Problems After an Abortion
(This could be the thesis statement of a persuasive essay that incorporates appeals to reason, appeals to emotion, opinions, and examples.)

Step Five: Write an outline or diagram.
1. Write the thesis statement at the top of the outline.
2. Write roman numerals I, II, and III on the left side of the page with A, B, and C under each numeral.
3. Next to each roman numeral, write down the best ideas you came up with in step three. These should all directly relate to and support the thesis statement.
4. Next to each letter write down information that supports that particular idea.

Step Six: Write the three supporting paragraphs.

Use your outline to write the three supporting paragraphs. Write down the main idea of each paragraph in sentence form. Do the same thing for the supporting points of information. Each sentence should support the paragraph of the topic. Be sure you have relevant and interesting details, facts, and quotes. Use transitions when you move from idea to idea to keep the text fluid. Sometimes, although not always, paragraphs can include a concluding or summary sentence that restates the paragraph's argument.

Step Seven: Write the introduction and conclusion.
See the exercise in Essay Three for information on writing introductions and conclusions.

Step Eight: Read and rewrite.
As you read, check your essay for the following:
- Does the essay maintain a consistent tone?
- Do all sentences serve to reinforce your general thesis or your paragraph theses?
- Do all paragraphs flow from one to the other? Do you need to add transition words or phrases?
- Have you quoted from reliable, authoritative, and interesting sources?
- Is there a sense of progression throughout the essay?
- Does the essay get bogged down in too much detail or irrelevant material?
- Does your introduction grab the reader's attention?
- Does your conclusion reflect back on any previously discussed material or give the essay a sense of closure?
- Are there any spelling or grammatical errors?

Tips on Writing Effective Persuasive Essays

✔ You do not need to include every detail about your subject. Focus on the most important ones that support your thesis statement.

✔ Vary your sentence structure. Avoid repeating yourself.

✔ Maintain a professional, objective tone of voice. Avoid sounding uncertain or insulting.

✔ Anticipate what the reader's counterarguments may be and answer them.

✔ Use sources that state facts and evidence.

✔ Avoid assumptions or generalizations without evidence.

✔ Aim for clear, fluid, well-written sentences that together make up an essay that is informative, interesting, and memorable.

Section Three: Supporting Research Material

Abortion Facts and Statistics

Editor's Note: These facts can be used in reports or papers to reinforce or add credibility when making important points or claims.

Abortion in America

- Since the 1973 legalization of abortion in the United States, over 40 million abortions have been performed.
- About 1.2 million abortions are performed in the United States each year.
- Abortion is the most frequent surgery performed in the United States.
- 89 percent of U.S. abortions occur in the first trimester of pregnancy.
- 98 percent of U.S. abortions occur during the first twenty weeks of pregnancy.
- 1 percent of U.S. abortions occur in the last trimester of pregnancy.
- The annual abortion rate of U.S. women aged 15–40 is 21 per 1,000 women.
- About 35 percent of all American women will have an abortion in their lifetimes.
- 25 percent of all pregnancies in the United States end in abortion.
- 87 percent of all U.S. counties have no abortion provider.
- 6 out of 10 American teens in states that have no parental consent laws say that one or more parents knew about their abortion.

Abortion Around the World

- Each year, 46 million women worldwide have abortions; 20 million of them are illegally obtained.

- The worldwide rate of abortion is 35 per 1,000 women.
- About 78,000 of the 600,000 pregnancy-related deaths occurring each year around the world are caused by unsafe abortions.
- About 60 abortions occur for every 100 women over the course of their reproductive lives.
- About half of all women who are having an abortion today are having their second abortion. One out of every five is having her third.
- According to the National Breast Cancer Coalition, the American Cancer Society, and the World Health Organization, no link between abortion and breast cancer has been established.
- In developing nations about 330 deaths occur for each 100,000 abortions.
- In developed nations 0.2 to 1.2 deaths occur per 100,000 abortions.

American Public Opinion on Abortion

- According to the opinion research organization Public Agenda, 66 percent of Americans believe that abortion should be legal in the first three months of pregnancy.
- The National Opinion Research Center reports that 15 to 26 percent of Americans believe that abortion should be permitted in the second trimester, and that 7 to 13 percent of Americans believe that abortion should be permitted in the third trimester.
- A 2002 Gallup poll contends that 24 percent of Americans believe that abortion should be legal in all cases.
- 78 percent of Americans feel that abortion is a woman's choice, despite their own personal opinion on the procedure, according to Gallup.
- Two years after the procedure, 72 percent of surveyed women remain satisfied with their decision to have an abortion, according to Gallup.

Finding and Using Sources of Information

No matter what type of essay you are writing, it is necessary to find information to support your point of view. You can use sources such as books, magazine articles, newspaper articles, and online articles.

Using Books and Articles

You can find books and articles in a library by using the library's computer or cataloging system. If you are not sure how to use these resources, ask a librarian to help you. You can also use a computer to find many magazine articles and other articles written specifically for the Internet.

You are likely to find a lot more information than you can possibly use in your essay, so your first task is to narrow it down to what is likely to be most usable. Look at book and article titles. Look at book chapter titles, and examine the book's index to see if it contains information on the specific topic you want to write about. (For example, if you want to write about the pros or cons of using RU-486, the abortion pill, and you find a book about abortion, check the chapter titles and index to be sure it contains information about RU-486 before you check out the book.)

For a five-paragraph essay, you do not need a great deal of supporting information, so quickly try to narrow down your materials to a few good books and magazine or Internet articles. You do not need dozens. You might even find that one or two good books or articles contain all the information you need.

You probably do not have time to read an entire book, so find the chapters or sections that relate to your topic, and skim these. When you find useful information, copy it onto a notecard or notebook. You should look for supporting facts, statistics, quotations, and examples.

Using the Internet

When you select your supporting information, it is important that you evaluate its source. This is especially important with information you find on the Internet. Because nearly anyone can put information on the Internet, there is as much bad information as good information online. Before using Internet information—or any information— try to determine whether the source seems to be reliable. Is the author or Internet site sponsored by a legitimate organization? Is it from a government source? Does the author have any special knowledge or training relating to the topic you are looking up? Does the article give any indication of where its information comes from?

Using Your Supporting Information

When you use supporting information from a book, article, interview, or other source, there are three important things to remember:

1. *Make it clear whether you are using a direct quotation or a paraphrase.* If you copy information directly from your source, you are quoting it. You must put quotation marks around the information and tell where the information comes from. If you put the information in your own words, you are paraphrasing it.

Here is an example of using a quotation:

> According to one author, "State lawmakers have enacted legislation requiring minor women to involve their families in decisions regarding the women's reproductive health. Some require the minor to obtain consent from a parent; others require physicians to notify minors' parents of the women's intent to terminate a pregnancy."
> (Hanson).

Here is an example of a brief paraphrase of the same passage:

> According to Georgana Hanson, states often require families to be involved in a young woman's decision about her pregnancy. In some cases she must receive parental consent; in other cases her doctor is required to inform her parents of the abortion.

2. *Use the information fairly.* Be careful to use supporting information in the way the author intended it. For example, it is unfair to quote an author as saying, "Abortion should not be legal," when he or she intended to say, "Abortion should not be legal in the last three months of pregnancy." This is called taking information out of context. This is using supporting evidence unfairly.

3. *Give credit where credit is due.* Giving credit is known as citing. You must use citations when you use someone else's information, but not every piece of supporting information needs a citation.
   - If the supporting information is general knowledge—that is, it can be found in many sources—you do not have to cite your source.
   - If you directly quote a source, you must cite it.
   - If you paraphrase information from a specific source, you must cite it.

If you do not use citations where you should, you are plagiarizing—or stealing—someone else's work.

Citing Your Sources

There are a number of ways to cite your sources. Your teacher will probably want you to do it in one of three ways:
   - Informal: As in the examples in number 1 above, you tell where you got the information in the same place you use it.
   - Informal list: At the end of the article, place an unnumbered list of the sources you used. This tells

the reader where, in general, you got your information.

- Formal: Use a note. An endnote is generally placed at the end of an article or essay, although it may be located in different places depending on your teacher's requirements.

Work Cited

Hanson, Georgana. "State by State, Chipping Away at Reproductive Rights." *Network News* Sept.–Oct. 2003.

Using MLA Style to Create a Works Cited List

You will probably need to create a list of works cited for your paper. These include materials that you quoted from, relied heavily on, or consulted to write your paper. There are several different ways to structure these references. The following examples are based on Modern Language Association (MLA) style, one of the major citation styles used by writers.

Book Entries

For most book entries you will need the author's name, the book's title, where it was published, what company published it, and the year it was published. This information is usually found on the inside of the book. Variations on book entries include the following:

A book by a single author:
> Guest, Emma. *Children of AIDS: Africa's Orphan Crisis.* London: Sterling, 2003.

Two or more books by the same author:
> Friedman, Thomas L. *From Beirut to Jerusalem.* New York: Doubleday, 1989.
> ———. *The World Is Flat: A Brief History of the Twentieth Century.* New York: Farrar, Straus and Giroux, 2005.

A book by two or more authors:
> Pojman, Louis P., and Jeffrey Reiman. *The Death Penalty: For and Against.* Lanham, MD: Rowman & Littlefield, 1998.

A book with an editor:
> Friedman, Lauri S., ed. *At Issue: What Motivates Suicide Bombers?* San Diego: Greenhaven, 2004.

Periodical and Newspaper Entries

Entries for sources found in periodicals and newspapers are cited a bit differently than books. For one, these sources usually have a title and a publication name. They also may have specific dates and page numbers. Unlike book entries, you do not need to list where newspapers or periodicals are published or what company publishes them.

An article from a periodical:
> Snow, Keith Harmon. "State Terror in Ethiopia." *Z Magazine* June 2004: 33–35.

An unsigned article from a periodical:
> "Broadcast Decency Rules." *Issues & Controversies On File* 30 Apr. 2004.

An article from a newspaper:
> Constantino, Rebecca. "Fostering Love, Respecting Race." *Los Angeles Times* 14 Dec. 2002: B17.

Internet Sources

To document a source you found online, try to provide as much information on it as possible, including the author's name, the title of the document, the date of publication or of last revision, the URL, and your date of access.

A Web source:
> Shyovitz, David. "The History and Development of Yiddish." Jewish Virtual Library 30 May 2005 < http://www.jewishvirtuallibrary.org/jsource/History/yiddish.html >.

Your teacher will tell you exactly how information should be cited in your essay. Generally, the very least information needed is the original author's name and the name of the article or other publication.

Be sure you know exactly what information your teacher requires before you start looking for your supporting information so that you know what to include with your notes.

Sample Essay Topics

Abortion Is Ethical

Abortion Is Unethical

Life Begins at Conception

Life Does Not Begin at Conception

Life Begins in the First Weeks of Pregnancy

Life Begins at Birth

Abortion Harms Women's Health

Abortion Is Safe

Access to Abortion Should Be Restricted

Access to Abortion Should Not Be Restricted

The Abortion Pill Is Safe

The Abortion Pill Is Unsafe

Women Face Emotional Problems After an Abortion

Women Do Not Face Severe Emotional Problems After an Abortion

Late-Term Abortions Should Be Legal

Late-Term Abortions Should Be Illegal

Organizations to Contact

Advocates for Youth
2000 M St. NW, Suite 750
Washington, DC 20036
(202) 419-3420
e-mail: questions@advocatesforyouth.org
Web site: www.advocatesforyouth.org

Advocates for Youth creates programs and policies that help young people make informed and responsible decisions about their reproductive and sexual health. Its publications include the fact sheets "Adolescents and Abortion," and "Peer Education: Promoting Healthy Behaviors."

Alan Guttmacher Institute (AGI)
120 Wall St., 21st Fl.
New York, NY 10005
(212) 248-1111
e-mail: info@guttmacher.org
Web site: www.agi-usa.org
The Alan Guttmacher Institute is a reproduction research group that advocates the right to safe and legal abortion.

American Life League (ALL)
PO Box 1350
Stafford, VA 22555
(540) 659-4171
e-mail: office@all.org
Web site: www.all.org

ALL promotes traditional family values and opposes abortion. It produces educational materials, books, and programs for pro-family organizations that oppose abortion.

Americans United for Life (AUL)

310 S. Peoria St., Suite 300
Chicago, IL 60607-3534
(312) 492-7234
e-mail: info@aul.org
Web site: www.unitedforlife.org

AUL promotes legislation to make abortion illegal. It operates a library and a legal resource center for such subjects as abortion, infanticide, destructive embryo research, and human cloning.

Center for Bio-Ethical Reform (CBR)

PO Box 219
Lake Forest, CA 92609
(949) 206-0600
e-mail: cbr@cbrinfo.org
Web site: www.cbrinfo.org

CBR opposes legal abortion, focusing its arguments on abortion's moral aspects. The center's Genocide Awareness Project (GAP) is a traveling photo-mural exhibit that visits university campuses to make students aware of the broader aspects of abortion.

Center for Reproductive Rights

120 Wall St.
New York, NY 10005
(917) 637-3600
e-mail: info@reprorights.org
Web site: www.crlp.org

The center advocates for safe and affordable contraception as well as safe and legal abortion for women worldwide. Its publications include "What if *Roe* Fell?" and *The Women of the World: Laws and Policies Affecting Their Reproductive Lives.*

NARAL Pro-Choice America

1156 Fifteenth St. NW, Suite 700

Washington, DC 20005
(202) 973-3000
e-mail: naral@naral.org
Web site: www.naral.org

NARAL Pro-Choice America works to develop and sustain a pro-choice political constituency in order to maintain the right of all women to legal abortion. The league briefs members of Congress and testifies at hearings on abortion and related issues.

National Right to Life Committee (NRLC)
512 Tenth St. NW
Washington, DC 20004
(202) 626-8800
e-mail: nrlc@nrlc.org
Web site: www.nrlc.org

NRLC is one of the largest organizations opposing abortion. It is promoting a constitutional amendment granting embryos and fetuses the same right to life as already-born persons, and it advocates alternatives to abortion, such as adoption.

Planned Parenthood Federation of America (PPFA)
434 W. Thirty-third St.
New York, NY 10001
(212) 541-7800
e-mail: communications@ppfa.org
Web site: www.plannedparenthood.org

PPFA is a national organization that supports people's right to make their own reproductive decisions without governmental interference. It provides contraception, abortion, and family-planning services at clinics throughout the United States.

Bibliography

Books

Burke, Theresa, *Forbidden Grief: The Unspoken Pain of Abortion*. Springfield, IL: Acorn, 2002.

Ehrlich, Shoshanna, *Who Decides? The Abortion Rights of Teens*. Westport, CT: Praeger, 2006.

Feldt, Gloria, *Behind Every Choice Is a Story*. Denton: University of North Texas Press, 2004.

Hendershott, Anne, *The Politics of Abortion*. New York: Encounter, 2006.

Jacob, Krista, *Our Choices, Our Lives: Unapologetic Writings on Abortion*. Lincoln, NE: iUniverse, 2004.

Klusendorf, Scott, *Pro-Life 101: A Step-by-Step Guide to Making Your Case Persuasively*. Signal Hill, CA: Stand to Reason, 2002.

Kreeft, Peter, *Three Approaches to Abortion: A Thoughtful and Compassionate Guide to Today's Most Controversial Issue*. San Francisco: Ignatius, 2002.

Saletan, William, *Bearing Right: How Conservatives Won the Abortion War*. Berkeley and Los Angeles: University of California Press, 2003.

Sanger, Alexander, *Beyond Choice: Reproductive Freedom in the 21st Century*. New York: Public Affairs, 2004.

Wagner, Teresa R., ed., *Back to the Drawing Board: The Future of the Pro-Life Movement*. South Bend, IN: St. Augustine's, 2003

Periodicals

Baumgardner, Jennifer, "We're Not Sorry, Charlie," *Nation*, February 2, 2004.

Cooney, Eleanor, "The Way It Was," *Mother Jones*, September/October 2004.

Economist, "The War That Never Ends—Abortion in America," January 18, 2003.

Gorney, Cynthia, "Imagine a Nation Without *Roe v. Wade,*" *New York Times,* February 27, 2005.

Halloran, Liz, "Abortion Wars, Once Again," *U.S. News & World Report,* December 5, 2005.

Harper, Jennifer, "Post-Abortion Trauma Seen as Worse than Miscarriages," *Washington Times,* December 13, 2005.

Head, Jeanne E., and Laura Hussey, "Does Abortion Access Protect Women's Health?" *World and I,* June 2004.

Issues and Controversies On File, "Abortion: Parental Consent Laws," June 24, 2005.

Johnson, Carolyn A., "Life, Death, and Partial-Birth Abortion," *Seattle Post-Intelligencer,* December 5, 2003.

Lerner, Sharon, "The Fetal Frontier," *Village Voice,* December 8–14, 2004.

Limbaugh, David, "The Mall of Shame," *Human Events,* May 3, 2004.

McQuade, Deirdre A., "*Roe's* False Freedom," *Wanderer,* November 17, 2005.

Quindlen, Anna, "Life Begins at Conversation," *Newsweek,* November 29, 2004.

Scheller, Christine A., "A Laughing Child in Exchange for Sin," *Christianity Today,* February 13, 2004.

Stein, Lisa, "An Undue Burden," *U.S. News & World Report,* June 14, 2004.

Vanwey, Erin, Brittany Canady, and Kristen Goldsmith, "What Do These Three Girls Have in Common . . ." *Teen People,* May 1, 2004.

Wall Street Journal "Abortion and the Law," November 5, 2005.

Wildman, Sarah, "Abort Mission," *American Prospect,* January 2004.

Web Sites

Abortion Facts and Information (www.abortionfacts.com). A pro-life Web site that provides links to similar sites, it includes a refutation of the most common pro-choice arguments.

Abortion—Just Facts (www.justfacts.com/abortion.htm). This site presents a list of relevant facts about the abortion debate, including details from significant court cases occurring over the past forty years.

Ethics Updates: Abortion and Ethics (http://ethics.san diego.edu/Applied/Abortion/index.asp). This site offers dozes of links to articles, legal documents, and audio interviews on the subject of abortion.

Index

Picture Credits

Cover: Brendan Smialowski/EPA/Landov
Maury Aaseng, 35
AP/Wide World Photos, 13, 14, 20, 24, 26, 36, 46
Carrie Devorah/WENN/Landov, 29
Justin Sullivan/Getty Images, 48
Kimberly White/Reuters/Landov, 42
© Katy Winn/CORBIS, 18

About the Editor

Mary E. Williams earned a master's in fine arts degree from San Diego State University, where she studied comparative literature, poetry, and creative writing. Williams has an enduring interest in race relations, world religions, and social justice. An editor for Greenhaven Press since 1996, she lives in San Marcos, California, with her husband, Kirk Takvorian.